D1319260

A Woman

of

Property

ALSO BY ROBYN SCHIFF

Revolver

Worth

A Woman

of

Property

Robyn Schiff

PENGUIN POETS

PENGUIN BOOKS

An imprint of Penguin Random House LLC

375 Hudson Street

New York, New York 10014

penguin.com

LIBRARY OF CONGRESS CATALOGING-IN-PUBLICATION DATA

Names: Schiff, Robyn, author.

Title: A woman of property / Robyn Schiff.

Description: New York, New York : Penguin Books, [2016] | Series: Penguin Poets

Identifiers: LCCN 2015048702 (print) | LCCN 2016001989 (ebook) |
    ISBN 9780143128274 (paperback) | ISBN 9780698407343 (ebook)

Subjects: | BISAC: POETRY / American / General.

Classification: LCC PS3619.C365 A6 2016 (print) | LCC PS3619.C365 (ebook) |
    DDC 811/.6—dc23

Printed in the United States of America

10 9 8 7 6 5 4 3 2 1

Set in Walbaum MT

Designed by Ginger Legato

CONTENTS

A Woman
of
Property

GATE

Everyone has a cousin Benjamin Bunny.
Peter said a walk would do him good.
The edge of the wood. Peter did not
enjoy himself anymore. He never would
again. The brooding lettuces
in their falcon hoods. The coppice gate

wound shut by weeds, the jaws of life
trying to keep it closed tight
but anyone can climb it.
As a child I played on a gate
in a neighborhood park
that swung of itself

and sounded like the distress
call of a rabbit. I stood on the bottom slat
and backed in and out of
the air. I'll never get out of here.
The gate was pure folly, without
fencing on either side,

Greek tragedy
staged around a doorway
the imagination strains to enter.
I was raised in an aisle seat
with an eye line of an actor
about to come through

from behind it. Melodramatic
onions grew wild.
I cried and cried until someone said
it's okay to cry,
it means the onions
are fresh. Every dream begins

with a threshold.
Meat in the driveway
where dogs tipped the garbage.
Where's your mouth? There is a whistle
you can buy that makes the sound
of a rabbit screaming

hunters use to call
whatever they want
out of the thicket
because everything they want
wants rabbit for dinner.
Move your hand

along the shaft to change
the call from jack to cotton-
tail and back again.
Once you see them nose
out of the interior at your bidding
what stops you from sounding

every single day? All day? The shrill
imagined rabbit's
canned terror. You can do it
with a reed of grass. Cup your hands.
Everything alive
is listening. I knew a hunter

who could do a spot-on fawn
whose suffering
would bring a doe
into the open every time.
He didn't want a doe, though.
He wanted a buck.

Here's what I can't stand
to acknowledge:
when bucks hear
the sound of the fawn
my friend makes with his mouth
they come, too, not in pity, but in lust,

so badly they want the doe
drawn by the yearning
of a fawn in need of her.
Everything is within range
suddenly, and who am I to judge.
He mounts her relief

and spring comes.
No. He takes
a bullet. I was caught
up in theatrics
and forgot whose
theater this is.

H1N1

God knows how our neighbors manage to breathe.
No one is allowed
to touch me

for infection is a hazard of mercy
I will not transmit
as Legion transcribed from the mouth

of Error into his body
and sent into a herd of swine
who sent it to the sea

who's been trying to return
to earth since creation
and nearly succeeds every day.

I just took my temperature.
98 degrees. I am better than healthy.
I am cooling even as the earth

heats, even as it meets the sea
further inland and negotiates
distance from increasingly

disadvantaged position. I
am cooling because nothing
touches me.

Others may go to the petting zoo
and country fair
but don't even tell me what they touch

there. I'm taking my temperature again;
my thermometer is digital and pink
and its beep is my name

being read from the book of life,
which is available on Kindle
and allows me to avoid the public library

but contains peculiar punctuation
errors and is transcribed by
evangelists while they wait

in line at gates you can't see from here. 98.5.
Still cooler than life. I have another
glass of water, and feel you turning in me,

my little book, flipping over and over.
It's time for bed, little sow, little sow.
The book of death is open on my bedside

table and is called *The Pregnancy
Countdown*, and contains "advice from the
trenches" about how to level

the enemy, the body.
It's time for bed, little bee, little bee. I open my window
and find ten dead between the pane and the screen,

which apparently has tears big enough
to enter and I leave them in state
in a pile and watch

the wind lift their
mighty wings in deathly
aspiration. It is the beginning

of flu season, Rosh Hashanah.
Every tear is recorded. I say *tear*
to rhyme with the chair by my window,

not *tear* to rhyme with the fear of God
here at the Fair of God
where the just

leer at the milk cow
and brush up against
captivity and slaughter

in the name of zoonosis
and the vector. Nothing touches me,
little scale, little scale,

I will not be meted, I will
not give the mosquito
her share even though the blood meal

is all she has to nurture her eggs
and mother-to-mother I hear
her flight even as she's drawn

to my breath by fate and nature,
which are one and as interchangeable
as babies in soap operas. Dangerous angel,

I will not lie down
with the lamb who is
contagious. I will not

hear your name recalled for I
have not named you and fear
tempers my love of the letters

of this world which are as
pins through the body
while the wings flail, but I

will not fail to meet you
when you get here
with your shadow

attached and your
failure a promise
entering the success

of your first breath. On what
grounds, on what faith,
dare we aspire

together where Legion
hears the ventilator
and enters the wire?

NURSERY FURNITURE

Today I am expecting a new chair.
I returned four this year
already. They were all *Sand*
with *Sand* piping and come from
a shop called the Land of Nod, where Alison,
the manager who deals with me,
gave me a gift certificate I am afraid
to redeem. Wary of what dream?
Nod does mean sleep,

but only as a pun on the state Cain
fled to after slaying
Abel—a waking sleep part
denial, part self-righteous,
a neutralizing hallucination of
North Carolina I rock in-
to inhaling the off-gassing batting, bare heels
rhythmically worrying a loose
staple behind

the rigid skirt at chair-bottom where coarse
temporary fiber
as permeable as loose
landscape fabric partitions
against interior interior where
an involuting spring grinds the
slow industrial rattle I recorded for
Alison and played back over
the telephone.

The Return Policy at Land of Nod,
like an insidious,
mum extension of the dead-
line for completion of a
project I wish I had not undertaken,
threatens endless, unrelenting
replacement of everything, no questions asked; but
Alison asked as courtesy
so I pushed the

game, equilateral public mouth
the tri-lipped angel of post-
traumatic repetition
contorts to foretell the past,
and listened, with Alison, to the estate
sale auctioneer's lamentation
rise as the runners rock, wind water riving deep
natural boundaries between kin;
original

keen of first material; the wood; the
block; the ax; the altar;
the kid. *This wasn't here when
I put the chair down last week,*
a delivery man said of a screw he
found beneath the skirt, lifting up
the chair to replace it the second time. *The chair
rejected it*

when you rocked the baby, didn't it? That's
the turn of the screw in
the other direction. I
hear the loosening of an
elemental hinge. I feel the torque spinning
in reverse up a helical
ridge. A pair of deliverymen had let them-
selves in, while I was sleeping, with
a skeleton

key. I held the ideal steel coil to the
light and saw the spiral
staircase out of the machine
the clematis in my yard
unwinds up along its own concertina
wire, wheeling soft turbines up the
porch screen like cammed hexes assisting ascension
of what foot leaving a sprocket
in digital

dream of pure soul what right have I to hold,
tame as it is, though it
looks wild? The earth wants my house
back. Smell its need in my base-
ment if you visit when tornado sirens
roll exultant maybes through a
yellow storm, but who wants a spirit back any-
more? I don't know why they ever
did. Are you still

there, Alison? Alison: I talk to
a lot of new mothers.
Me: So? Alison: There is
something you can take for that,
but you cannot get it here. Me: I just want
return without replacement. When
the lyric makes me sing what I did not even
want said, to get to stop having
to keep thinking

it. Abandonment is a legal quest-
(Mid-word? The call was dropped.)
Later via text: r u
more afraid of beauty or
infinity? Did u come up here 4 the
view or the drop? To watch the self-
mutilated spider pace the scale or, on the
other bright pan, flashing the sun
back at the sun

in full white expanse like the disk head of
an ancient god or the
cool and luminous earthlit
moon, a strobe I control the
intensity of just by turning on and
off my bedside lamp, most tender
infinitesimal measure taken in the
history of time meted in
insomniac

dawngloam lightspeed, minus one dark fissure
portending damnation
in mirrors—this freehand one-
line torso floating beneath
gallows in a one-guess death-match of hangman
interruptus—the severed eighth
autotomized leg of that same spider twitching
out a few hot counts, then nothing
doing until

Judgment. Surely adjudication will
not be made of the few
losses I cut; after all,
I did not eat the fish I
freed—not the radiant stone-winged sea robin
I hooked and released in nauseous
dread with the help of the only friend my father
had, who upended it in calm
didactic sea-

showmanship ennobled by indifferent
mercy so out could swim
a still-living meal of three
black pink backlit shrimp before
returning them all in one hand to the depths
of the reuptaking Sandy
Hook Bay. In the flashing grid of shadow cast by
rigs passing over the slatted
bridge under which

we'd anchored, the bottom-feeder and the
very bottom are still
pulsing on the bow of *My
Compassion*, a transparent
craft I steer in memory with the motor
off in no-wake waters. Inquest.
Inform. Inscape. In absentia. Grace under
surveillance is etiquette. Guests
come and go and

I rest my rest on the baby's head which
has an opening and
consider Justice. The First
Mistake was issuing her
a two-pan balance. Remember offsetting
the equilibrium of the
peaceable kingdom at the head of the crib. I
brought it home from the Land of Nod
eager to hang

four animals around a fifth: wolf, worm,
lion, lamb, and monkey,
and sat down and wept at the
problem of how to center
the new world. Likewise some call the head of the
crib its foot. The room stays put, but
the whole world turns around it. *Bury this screw with
haste*, the delivery man
told me; and I

felt the vibration of the drilling of
corresponding pilot
holes pre-fitted to accept
everything I love. *Where?* she
asked. *Under the house,* he said. *How deep?* she asked.
Deeper than you think, he said. *With
what?* she asked. *An earthworm digs with its mouth,* he said.
When I envision the soul and
body I feel

aeration of the soil. Mechanics meets
telekinesis in
a power tool called Will. You
turn it on by saying "No."
It's not true both parts of a severed earthworm
both grow back, but since as a child
I believed it so, imagine with me splitting and
splitting each living fork; you aren't
thinking if you

don't think all the way down with every worm.
Part those and those. Think it
with a real blade, now.

FOURTH OF JULY, 2012

I remember a performance
of Antigone in which she
threw herself on the floor of
the universe and picked up
a piece of dust. Is that
the particle? It startled me.
Was it Scripted? Directed?
Driven? I am a girl, Antigone.
I have a sister. We love
each other terribly. I am a woman
of property. The milk of the footlights.
The folds of the curtain. I remember
a performance of Antigone. She stooped.
There was a wild particle.
It was glorified by my distance.
I heard the hooves of the dust.
The ticking of the script
calibrating oblivion. I saw
the particle hanging
and Antigone needed something
to do with her hands
and she did it.

A DOE REPLACES IPHIGENIA
ON THE SACRIFICIAL ALTAR

There was a need
to be weak and I met
it. I appeared in the confusion
between strength and
surrender, as if out of nowhere,
that's the illusion.
I was reared
ruminating
in a thicket of
sorrow with a beautiful
string of drool
hanging out the side of my
mouth like a loose
phosphorescent
tether.
How will I know
what to do, I wondered.
No one does, my mother said.
And then, as the drawing back of the ocean
before a tsunami
suddenly exposes
outrageous fish on the seabed, gasping,
a great inhalation placed me
here panting on the sacred grass.
I feel like a girl in heaven,
but I am a beast in a clearing.
I came to
as the wind picked up
and in the bay
as the tide
came in,

what a blow to mankind,
an animalcrude wind
to war, toward
war, untoward
toward war
took my breath
away with it.

A HEARING

When my neighbor, a cult leader, asked if
he could cultivate the
strip of earth on his side of
my drive, about half the width
of my drive, with a depth unknown to me, and
which in all honesty I did
not know I owned, how not concede what I'd declined
already?   *Are you saying you*
consented?   Not

exactly.   *But you said "Yes"*   I didn't say
"No."   *Plaintiff claims the strip*
of earth was "unsightly."   It
unsighted him from sight of
me—unforeseen consequence of unsighting
myself from him. *So you're saying*
you grew a wall of weeds intentionally?   What
do you mean "grew"? I did not do
anything. I

was unaware, at the time, that it was
even my property.
                    There was no deed? Exactly.
                    There is no deed on record?
I didn't do anything.   *Exactly. Plaintiff*
claims neglect of property.   But
I don't do anything exactly. That's my way.
                    Driveway not in dispute.   I mean
my habit.   *Your*

habit or your practice? There's a difference;
that difference is motive.
I have no will. I have a
habitat that possesses
me that I overlook.   *Do you look after*
it?   Born so late in natural
history, I look after everything. Take care,
caretaker, I said to myself
at the closing,

there's a hoard in the root cellar of this
haven—old doors, window
frames, pitchforks, and two-by-fours
with nails driven through—with the
Readiness and the Already in their hone
and in their dust, in their bright rust
florets and in the interior rust of the
centennial lead water pipes
the whole stockpile

leans against that run brown water like the
internal bleeding of
a vendetta.   *What did you*
add to it?   Last night I propped
an empty poster frame and brittle sheet of
glass that fell suddenly from the
nursery wall that had contained a rhyme I nailed
too crudely, now I understand,
in the lath and

plaster, which couldn't bear the pounding I gave
it and in retrospect
should have been first entered with
a delicate bit. The rhyme
concerned the alphabet: *A* is for Aesop.
A bucket of water, a clock,
and an articulate swimming dog with something
clinging to its nape advanced a
mutual cause.

They saw the green strobe on the dock throb code
to the minutemen and
responded as planned.   *Aesop?*
I meant to say Atreus.
Motion to Strike from the Record   **Motion**   I
thought they were animals   **Denied**
There was a dog who recognized Agamemnon.
She was on a dung heap scratching
herself in her

sleep when he returned. Madame Bovary
is what I think they call
that same dog in hell Jane Eyre
recalled when she heard Mr.
Rochester's riderless black horse chained to the
furnace—   *Motion to Strike*   **Motion**
Denied   and I could already feel the epic
concealment of the shiv as I
leaned the broken

frame on the pile of weaponized wood in
the basement when a cool
foundational fug, like the
breath of a river stone, washed
my heart of panic. The boiler points down. Twice
a year I change its filter and
start over. Every time I descend the stairs I
trespass what I already own.
"I dreamed there was

no frame there," my son said when I laid him
down. A nightmare or a
wish? A wish or an omen?
An omen or a vision?
Was it literal or symbolic? Was it
this? "Good night" good night "Good night" good
night I turned off the light and watched TV until
I fell asleep. "It stresses the
root system, so

don't prune in a drought," the garden expert
warned the host; I turned the
channel to a hand in close-
up unzipping a loveseat
cushion. What tiny steel teeth the zipper had,
like the baby mouth of a doll-
house-scale figure of the hit man from *The Spy Who
Loved Me* whose carnal name I can't
put my finger

on—let's call him Orestes—and when the
hand tore a piece off the
yellow foam insert and fed
it to its chewing face with
such tenderness I remembered the dripping
dog, whose howling was a wind in
itself, wasn't a dog at all, so goes the joke,
but the first warlord's cursed earth wife
Clytaemestra

and the henchman who troubled Bond, whose one
speaking line was a toast
to love: Jaws. *Jaws 3-D*, the
abysmal surfacing of
mother love; the most powerful jaw in the
world is the one that sucks. Viper
is what Clytaemestra dreamed she held in her arms
but loved nonetheless. "All the ex-
ecutioners

plead that they act for just retribution. . . .
Every correction is
a blood-bath," I read in the
Oresteia, intro. Rich-
mond Lattimore. "Don't read that in bed," my hus-
band said. Okay, okay, I'll just
finish *Jude the Obscure*. Terrible children of
the modern world, a shark pup in
captivity

was nursed with a garden hose. "A voice of
fear deep in the house." The
resident on call in the
NICU, let's call her Evil-
Though-Well-Meaning, who inserted the feeding
tube and the spinal tap, said she
practiced on herself. "Here is my own soil that I
walk," said Orestes, but Fury
had to ask, "What

is this place, Athena, you say is mine?"
Deep fear with no bottom.
I stand in the basement but
the depth of my property
line fathoms the mantle toward a core of
freezing fire. "Bring me my burning
robe," Agamemnon said standing like a glacier
in the bathtub. Imagine the
color of the

filthy bathwater and the fetid black
wave he made when he fell
back down in it. Want to know
why my roses grow dead on
a living vine? Prayer against civil war: Let
us hate with a single heart. Don't
drink the runoff. I always wanted a ruin
so I bought a run-'er-down. Love
contaminates

love, I pray for my water
and was given a house-
cooling gift of black tulips
that are decapitated
every May. Imagine my fear when I saw
his hybrid daylilies burst through
my property. Hypocrite Marys, first, pared to
an accusatory finger
that splayed open

then like a self-flaying fish, a bachelor-
uncle's game of here is
the church and here's the steeple,
open the doors and see all
the people gassed in their seats by an unknown
chemical agent pumped through the
vents during something like a Russian rendition
of *Les Mis*, miserable die-
another-day

lilies whose theater is dispossession.
Winner of two Golden
Masks. What next? Swan boats? Do not
tempt the gods to board your craft.
You cannot get them off. The wilderness goes all
the way down and pulls the roots from
underneath. A white rush where the fire burns hottest,
a white rush, like a sacred hart
ex machina

so Artemis enters the gaping O
to console us all. It was a deer,
she tells Clytaemestra; a deer
on the altar; your daughter
lives; the wind is still;
and your father
is mortal.

DYED CARNATIONS

There's blue, and then there's blue.
A number, not a hue, this blue
is not the undertone of anyone
but there it is, primary.
I held the bouquet
in shock and cut the stems at a deadly angle.
I opened the toxic sachet of flower food
with my canine and rinsed my mouth.
I used to wash my hands and daydream.
I dreamed of myself and washed
my hands of everything. Easy math.
Now I can't get their procedure
at the florist off my mind.
The white flowers arrived! They overnighted
in a chemical bath
and now they have a fake laugh
that catches like a match
that starts the kind of kitchen fire
that is fanned by water.
They won't even look at me.
Happy Anniversary.

ALTHOUGH

              lobster is a delicacy to
lobster, and possessed of the ability
              to drop and grow back claws,
lobster is not known to feed off of

              itself. The temptations of self-sufficiency
are great, but not great
              enough, nor is it the practice to keep lobsters
in tanks decorated with seaweed and authentic

              rocks, harvest a claw at lunch, and let grow
back like a plant on the sill incrementally
              added to the pot, pet and lab and living menu
developing personality in time,

              although its face
never warms to mine, and if *face*
              is too strong a word—
it looks so like a terrible crack

              in a wall something worse is coming through—
unless it's the odor, the strong
              personality that's developing is
my own, and a better word for that is

              appetite. My town has no aquarium.
I go to the supermarket
              with a wild hunger to
observe. Cured ham should be sliced thin enough

to read the *Times* through. In line
at the deli counter on a day the door
        was wide open to the possibility of
early spring for which

        sacrifice was made
in the freezing dark a few weeks
        earlier, I saw
a thinly sliced rip of incandescent

        honeyed ham dangling
like the pendulum of a clock
        in the stringy grip of
a wasp. No, not *like* a pendulum.

        Not *like* a clock. I was young then
and mistook nearly everything.
        I have been carrying this for
a long time now.

It was a pendulum.
It was a clock.

GARDENING

In a place in the yard where nothing grows,
I lift the brick that's nothing's cornerstone
and unearth swarms of living dirt

passing what I thought was a moth
between them rip by rip, but it
was not, I came to see, a shared food;

it was their eggs. I found a nail and a hinge
in the mud, but no
gate. I found a hasp and a shell

and a slat. Not
feasting; reproducing. Not this;
that. Not division;

multiplication.
Not the catch; the hatch.
Ants blast downward

with the auger of cooperation
right through the single footstep
stamped like the sole

sole that so chilled Crusoe
it might as well have been cloven
by one brick

in the bed, joined by no others
in wall, path, stairway, or border,
first or last already or still

in formation, so
infested, so violently
solo, it must be the monumental

cold downed head of the framer
of some dull
concept, some pyramid

scheme, vacant slab-faced
antique statuary
whose squirming visage

faces the muck.
Worker ants craze the subterranean
emergency entrance whose surface name

is exit. Stampede, where units
are larger; trampling is the crisis
those of us with soft bodies

fear dismounting a slow escalator
that nevertheless outpaces
the interval between arriving

and arrival; one foot
on the grinder, one foot on
the landing, like being delivered

into my own body. Knowledge
and terror. Wake up, commuter,
your bottled water is throwing

beautiful spiteful rainbows all along the corridor.
Their bobbing is my radiance
and I can see forever, the crowds

and carnage of which no one
has gotten right save one location scout
who saw a day-lit mall where,

sadly patient, pressing a security gate
sacred as a choir screen,
bored, rotting, underpaid

supernumeraries
groan at the principals.
What's more revolting?

the informed runnel of carpenter ants
that erupted through a crack in my porch
to surround a living snail—they entered the shell

and took the spiral from within like
dutiful tourists up a spire; reformation
whitewashed twists lit by an unseen source; the

narrowness of passage; and imperceptible
to me, though I listened, the swoosh
of advancing ants already climbing

a staircase to the interior that the
snail no doubt sensed, if couldn't
hear. I saw its alien horns strain to

understand, like the ears of a dog—which—
watch my hands—lead me to
your second choice: wolf snail ravaging

common tree snail, shell and all.
There exists in nature
a wolf-kind of every species

whose criminal hunger takes the shape of
the most vile courtship; in this case,
the wolf slogs the viscid ectoplasm

of its victim; to watch it, it looks like
horrible walking, but
its lips are so elongated they are nearly

an appendage and it's eating
the contrail of the other snail even
as it's hunting it. Slow or fast, I can't say.

Pursuit staged by Patience
in revenge of the abduction of her child
by Time and Silence. I watched footage

of a wolf snail on a tree
snail on a muted big-screen TV
and thought they

must be mating until one just
disappeared entirely. There's a shill
and a shell and a shell man, sleight of hand,

a mark, and tremendous morose
marksmen from another scale, as among
us some have come from another time. The

simultaneity
sickens me. The overlaps. Wolf snail rewinding
common snail up its trembling spool,

the wheeling
of the whelk
inside the whelk.

The wave rolling
and the root we share below
the house. The wheel inside the

wheel inside the meal inside the meal of
our first date—snails you dared me with shame
of worldlessness to eat, but there was a third there—

a game statistician who's
since left a tenuous post
to enter the system. I eat nails now,

so acute is my deficiency of iron
and men. I eat soil. I put on
my gauntlets and plod out

with rake and hoe to work the beds,
but this garden has been working me.
It took me on the long con. Who

am I, a *tourist,*
to buy *here.* Was it so long ago
I took the steep enclosed spiral

staircase up the tower
in the walled medieval stronghold
and turned into

the occlusion. Levitation
is the name gravity takes
when the hourglass

is upside down,
but the hourglass
never is. Up and down

the corkscrew
go the angels in Jacob's vision.
Cheap revue

that plays in competition with
a cash-cum-slot machine
in the black box

lounge of the casino. *Know
I am with you,* Jacob heard God
whisper, *and will keep you*

*wherever you go, and will bring you
back to this land;
for I will not leave you*

until I have done
to you
what I have promised

to do.
Tourism
is the oldest industry;

dreaming is the oldest
tour. Every pilgrim has his scallop shell
to show for his. I live

in mine. Of the convergence
of the channel patterns carved
in calcium crystal, dry tributaries

that flow the half-shell to a single point,
I was told: Rejoice. You Are Not Alone, Pilgrim,
Even The Sea Maps Our Reunion On

The Very Shells It Scatters, but what
momentum
—look how the lines meet at broken

swinging muscle—
what horde pushed so
the hinge at the symbolic

intersection
of these symbolic lines in shell
the dead pilgrims followed

to their next symbolic lives
but which map just as well
the tendency of wolves

to merge packs; right now
deep in a Russian village
where they live on snow and horses,

wolves are coalescing.
I once stood by myself
in the ancient tragic scallop-shell-

shaped theater at Ephesus and saw
the flights of empty stairs
rush the stage.

The inverse
of a shooting star,
what I watched

was increments.
When my son dreams
the wolf snail

whose grave turning
has the clarity
of his grave purity

how can I tell him
it was just a dream?
I taught him

how to sleep
by putting him down
alone awake.

I taught him how
to count by starting with sheep
and staying there until

consciousness
altered the word.
A herd

eyes the narrowness
of the stile
from a great distance

but unbearable
supercolonies of ants
are not *contiguous*

in the human sense.
They are practical, though, and kick
up a layer of clay we form brick with

from the middle of the earth
where they are retreating in panic
with the eggs I saw them rolling

in their shining mandible
face hooks. And I dropped
the brick.

SIREN TEST

Crisis in absence, practice-howl tuning
its force, that old story
dragging a moralizing
wolf out of the matrix. Called
to the porch to picture the mouth. Every first
Wednesday of the month, if it's clear.
Why would you stop yourself? Who are you talking to?
Get back in the house. Where are you?
Pack counts off. Where

are you? Who are you with? Pitch modulates
mouth. It alters you to
make a sound like this; your face
takes an upstream mien like the
kype of an experienced fish whose muzzle
transforms into a monkey wrench.
How wide will he open his? How I admire an
animal who hunts with its face.
Unsportsmanlike

wolves plunging their grins in the salmon falls;
this is no sport and I
am no man. When a boy cries
wolf a wolf cries boy. The woods
behind my house only go back a few feet
and are lit by a commuter
train. Today is overcast but the siren churned
its test, nevertheless. It called
me to the porch

with a question. Do not ask if this is
practice, just get in the
basement and load some laundry,
then pack up the old wrapping
paper into the Rubbermaid containers
I bought to organize the gift
giving of the Magi. I give and give but won't
give up my position. Get back
in the house, I

said to myself, and made myself useful.
Sometimes I am thankless
and sometimes I am so full
of aimless gratitude it
is a curse some call love, some rumination,
when I just sit here all day all
night counting my unaccountables. I recall
my mother counting my fingers
once: *Since you have*

the same number on each, let's just count one
hand twice. Understand? Yes.
We proceeded to count off
aloud together each time
she touched the tip of one of my fingers with
her own index. I was six and
knew how many of every thing I had; I had
a feeling I was born with that
I descended

from a line of counting house witnesses
and already knew how
to keep a secret and a
list, yet my little hand shook
in my mother's hand as much as it had when
she once used her fingernails to
extract ten splinters from my palm and I withdrew
it just as fast when we came up
short upon my

thumb at only number nine as I would
many years hence from the
hired grip of a boardwalk
fortune-teller when she looked
at my palm and said, *A life well lived is worth*
even more than longevity.
What will be—the whole damned boardwalk gone; the wood, free—
will be. I dropped my last arcade
quarter between

those slats and accidentally turned on
the starving sea. I had
had enough anyway, my
mother had said. And so I
had. Saying "had had" like that reminds me to
recount to you how it was I
was led to miscount my fingers: You'll remember
my mother counting two tribes of
Indians on

one of my hands so won't be surprised to
learn she tricked me by by-
passing the pinky on the
second pass. As a child I
invented an internal system I called
to with my invoice whereby I
organized my time-sensitive material
according to the future date
on which action

is needed I much later learned is called
by clerks a "tickler file."
Underhanded phantom itch,
mine reckons ways of this world
with the next via a system of pulleys
threaded as the strategy to
sacrifice by proxy the sons of others in-
to a labyrinth zeros in-
evitably

in on one's own. Don't ask a mirror whose
head is on the coins that
feed this contraption, let's call
it "war," if you don't want to
know that the ashtray of every Toyota
in Jersey was full of metal
slugs we used instead of quarters on the Parkway,
but one man, let's call him "Daddy,"
had just one slug

tied to a thread. Don't move a finger if
you're playing dead. Present
and unaccounted for, my
purloined letter, steal yourself,
son, I'm teaching you how to make yourself in-
visible. "I only cry in-
side," he said, clearing the threshold into cold dis-
regard—the wind—which just standing
in was his first

career. Finite accounting, please lead me
to your zero that I
may begin my encounter.
Today I'm thinking of a
number. The sensitive boy who sensed the wolf
approaching. It was coming, but
it was not the truth yet. Do not hire a prophet
to do nearsighted work. It's not
the boy's fault you're

not ready for him. The moral is; Trust,
and trust's not trust until
its test. I counted on the
crying boy who swore he heard
the wash of piss against these trees we call ours.
I possess such unbearable
affection for my glistening property I
fear it will be unborne. The wolf
raises its leg

and shakes its mark over everything I
have. Now what? Cycle a
second load of wet laundry
through the infernal compact
Bosch clothes dryer, and fold, fold, fold; it's hotter
than a Whirlpool; be careful with
those snaps! What a long day already. Waiting for
the All Clear that shares its silence
with Continue

to Take Cover to distinguish itself
among the intervals
is rather like being kept
up all night on the Murphy
bed of friends straining my ears to discern a
difference between Tick and Tock
in an old test invented to determine the
sensitivity of angels,
and having it

dawn on me that though the censorious
princess kept awake by
that depressing leftover
pea passed an ancient test of
rank, she failed by far even more sensitive
character evaluation
by complaining to her host. She won't be asked back.
Earth is cruel; accommodations
scarce. Everything

keeps changing hands. If you put your host's clock
in the guest room drawer, take
it out before you go! Say
nothing but "Thank you!" I had
said "I had had enough," but I had not had.
Put another way: tick tick. Don't
treat fire drills like holy fire; treat holy fire the
way you would treat your own mother.
Intimately,

over a great distance you will never
overcome. Fear nothing,
I whispered to my child, but
to tell the truth: The moral
is. Here's a confession: The child you hired to
quietly confront the coming
wolf was born into my claim. I tried to hide him,
but all he wants is to be held
accountable.

I named him Wolf so he could cry himself
to sleep. It goes without
saying I want him to out-
live you, whoever you are.
If poems aren't for saying what goes without
saying, I don't know what they're for.
I don't know what I'm going to do tomorrow.
In crisis I stood in the cold
American

Museum of Natural History
and was briefly consoled
by the unnatural arts
of concealment by briefly
illuminating two hunting gray wolves by
pressing the white doorbell outside
their dark vitrine. "Who's there?" the wolves said. A dreadful,
fast vision flashed a terrified
peripheral

white-tailed deer against a blind spot on my
side of the glass. Its last
footfalls, cast in infamy
in the stride of extended
suspension, melt both the artificial snow
and my sad heart. The wolves said, "Whose
side are you on?" I don't know. An iron support
pole enters the point at which the
one leg touching

down feels the snow before being gathered
up again below the
running wolf. Conserve the earth
for the living dead. Let it
go, hums the blue light of the soul in flight. In
proper orientation with
Polaris, the Big Fucking Dipper sifts for some
thing of value.

A DOE DOES NOT REPLACE IPHIGENIA
ON THE SACRIFICIAL ALTAR

There was a need
to be weak and I met
it. I appeared in the confusion
between strength and
surrender, as if out of nowhere,
that's the illusion.
I was reared
ruminating
in a thicket of
sorrow with a beautiful
string of drool
hanging out the side of my
mother like a loose
phosphorescent
tether.
How will I know
what to do, I wondered.
No one does, my mouth said.
Don't touch me. I want to stand,
for once, on the bed
and flip the switch on the fan
that reverses the direction of
the blades myself
while the fan is moving.
It is a small switch, and I have a
small hand from which
an insignificant wind
is swinging in
the other direction now.

I feel like a beast in a clearing,
but I am a girl in heaven.
I passed out
as the wind picked up
and in the bay
as the tide
came in,
what a blow to mankind,
an automatic wind
to war, toward
war, untoward
toward war
took my breath
away with it.

AMERITHRAX

The pure spores of anthrax
                go forward
soilborne from the anthrax-
                dead, disturbed, vengeful,
engineered, natural,
                returning well rested, dormant time machine

reactivated,
                what say you of
eternity that doesn't concern
                unbearable turning versus
unbearable remaining, you still-there,
                where

duration and stasis meet
                in the carcass,
microscopic-zombie-
                boarding-the-envelope-again,
have I changed? I do not think I have. Have
                I changed?

Neither the damned
                nor the blessed
are said to feel time's passage, but something, call it *time*,
                felt me
while I was washing dishes once,
                and when I jumped, the glass

I dropped burst into a shimmer
                    of grit that lit the dustpan
as I swept it up: the iridescence
                    in soil,
the mica and
                    infinitesimal

crystal,
                    is joined by glass shattered
in fear and insistence
                    that that something otherwise recordless is
here in this sieve.
                    And today, twenty years later,

my baby
                    Sacha pointing "baby" "baby" "baby"
into every dark corner
                    makes me believe this
house of ours is infested
                    with the infant dead

infants sense with their
                    indiscriminate eyes
that are as accustomed to not as to is,
                    and which I
accessed once
                    by attending to a shadow cast

through the original
              front window
low on the living room
              wall that water appeared to be
pouring through and must have
              been the sweep of some second hand

whose anatomy is water, water,
              the basis of all life
and which had until
              this point been imperceptible
to me within me,
              liquid in

ambient conditions go we; not a shadow, no,
              I saw that day, but an
effulgence.
              It was Stunning. No
it was not stunning,
              it moves me still. Hand

that is not a hand,
              whose movement
is the standard for quartz,
              please hold still, and it was gone
to me. You know the Unicorn
              tapestries at the Cloisters? I

read about their restoration
              in what is known as a "wet lab";
no windows of course,
              a giant white tiled bath
like what I would erect
              at the holy

gates to autoclave that grin off
              the mouth of the bacteria
that's eating us alive.
              It's not actually mouths,
but a balance
              of enzymes that

absorb via passive transit,
              but you know what I mean,
and here, submerged in a few
              purified inches,
the rippling unicorn. Sacha
              only once

cried "baby" into darkness
              in fear. Passively
noted, generally,
              like flora we've seen before.
Monotony is the only
              way to survive

longevity. And you, Anthrax?
                    Hercules dips
his arrow in the blood
                    of the Hydra. Is it exciting?
It's just business.
                    You have not seen much

of the world, interstitial agent
                    who releases
the toxins
                    and drains out of the body
already asleep again
                    in the tragic black bleed that

is the tag of your presence,
                    weaving your life of action
and dormancy
                    like the ritualized surfacing
and submerging
                    of memory that the

repeating motifs of formal art
                    figure: disappearing; reappearing;
the very craft contriving
                    the Unicorn itself
rendered with
                    nimble

cool
           by medieval
weavers who stitched one inch an hour—
           a statistic shared in the source I
consulted to seem painstaking
           but feels breakneck to me

even in this fleet age and
           must have seemed
instantaneous then,
           a spontaneous generation of
living cloth mailed suddenly into space,
           pace

being the one detail time travelers
           comment on most.
And it's not just speed
           that's dangerous.
So many weavers die
           of inhalational anthrax

your street name is
           woolsorter's disease,
contracted by weavers
           as you waft dreaming off the soft
yarn and awaken
           furiously germinating in

the fell manner
            I can only imagine
I've seen mayflies mating
            in swarms
but this seething is nothing like coupling
            and takes more than seeing to

envision
            wilding, outnumbering,
uncontainable,
            uncontainable,
uncontainable, uncontainable,
            uncontainable,

uncontainable
            force in this house.

POSSESSION

Be careful backing up,
black truck.
This cul-de-sac
is wrapped around
a telephone pole
that was driven
through the median
as through a heart
and maybe it comes out
the other side in another
neighborhood at dawn,
not dusk, where gossip
is the truth
and the little girl
wheeling her bicycle
counterclockwise
around the pole we share
was gently plotted in
under the grid
of utility wires
still wearing her shirt
and shoes and smile
much opposed
to the child here
beneath a tangle of transmissions
that look like knots
I'll have to comb out later
and the soles of the feet
of which each bear two rows
of bike pedal bite marks
you can't rub out

and have to just wait on
to fade themselves
like the colt
she's riding
in her game of
heatstroke farm
whose ribs are showing
and has too many more rotations yet
to make around the axis of the
static world. Mr. Peterson,
the next-door neighbor,
is sitting on the folding chair
in his driveway. Hi, Mr. Peterson!
On Halloween he places a cardboard box
of the biggest candy bars money can buy
on his lap and you get to keep
whatever you can get out
a small hole he cut into the top.
It's time
to come in, Amy,
dinner's ready
and your brother,
who's been hiding
so long in the backseat of the car
while no one sought him
is hungry, hungry he
says for something other
than what your mother
tucked under a moist paper towel
in a microwave-safe dish. He has
the upper-body strength of a man

because he's been on metal crutches
for all seven years he's not been walking.
Before that he was a baby,
and they don't walk
at all. Last weekend
in the aboveground
swimming pool,
leveled by the moony
weightlessness,
he did the dead man's float
all day. Good. Better for me.
"Marco" and then nothing for an hour.
I'm saving up
for something big. I don't know
what. We'll have to somehow get
them to stay in
bed. It's hard when it's
still so bright outside.
What's in the mother's
nightstand? Jill and I
take it out every weekend
when the kids are sleeping
and poke at it like a dead animal
with the dull golf pencil the mother
underlines programs with
in the *TV Guide*. She watches
Falcon Crest and then
I guess she goes to sleep.
Who could possibly dream
in this heat? The oscillating fan
makes it sound like we're always

on a runway and just freezes
the sweat to our faces, and each
bead on the children's long weird
necks has a grain of sandbox sand in it.
When the fan turns from them
it looks like tears
the Sphinx would shed
are running down
their torsos and arms.
Our voices bleat
into the blades.
We just say
our own names
over and over.
Not a runway,
a slaughterhouse.

THE MOUNTAIN LION

In combination
of undulation
        and the gait of a worm,
        the "soft robot," comprised of pneumatic valves,
            gasps to ripple itself below the two-
            centimeter-high limbo

stick, slit that stands in
this simulation
        for a jagged crevice
        in the shifting bricks of a city on fire
            into which mad human desire but no
            human hand can reach for you,

and appears as a
breach of horizon
        by a foggy, breathed-on
        vulcanized glass X, whose locomotion is
            breath; who creeps on its lungs; aspiration
            tenor and vehicle both

moving me; Wild
Spirit; lab child;
        wind prophecy; low, low
        under the limbo with it; and now what new
            low, newer and lower, what new will I
            do and who will I do it

to? On a recon
mission, speeding on
       hyperventilation.
       On all fours with X passing under the bridge
            of sighs, neither faceup, facedown, foot- or
            headfirst, orientation

nothing to Crisscross,
implicit promise
       in the design of X
       that progress waits in the direction X is
            progressing on its all-limb signature-
            of-the-team-of-engineers

X-mark crossing be-
neath the line that the
       signatures of mortals
       rest upon. No rest for the engineered whose
            sleep is powering up. Nature's torpid
            hibernating monster, whose

overwintering
in rot makes it spring
       desperately from its log,
       bloodquesting vectoring mother of Grendel
            from the illuminate muck of a lake
            lair ferocious on the make,

is the prototype
of the power-light
                on X that indicates
                a readiness as well honed as the mouthparts
                        time and nature equipped the mosquito
                        female with, cheapest bio-

weapon, exporting
itself both on wings
                and trade in used tires
                to bring arthropod-borne viruses the world
                        over. This is the Infiltration Age.
                        To be made in the likeness

of Nature is to
be inserted. So
                enters a field mouse through
                the wiring of my house. The posture of
                        supplication is interposition.
                        Where the head goes the body

follows. He made his;
we make ours; his raids;
                ours raids. I saw a mouse
                bring the other half of my saltine to her
                        mouth. There's the ant poison ants deliver
                        unbeknownst to their queen. No

such bait exists for
mice. No such queen. Each
              trap traps one mouse. I set
              two myself with the butter knife I made my
                        lunch with to bait the catch and slide them way
                        under the oven before

heading back down to
the basement to pack
              a picnic in the locked
              compartment under the rubber trunk mat of
                        the avenging backfit competitive
                        driverless easy-out

vehicle I was
called by the darkness
              to invent. Appalling
              invitational I qualified for at
                        seventeen when I woke up in my car
                        in someone's living room I

have been living in
since with my hands at
              ten and two clocking the
              stasis. Driverless vehicles of future
                        regret compelled by the semi-active
                        passive suspension ghost ride

the Möbius test
track searching the dust
        for survivors and feed-
        back. Get back in the car. There's an electric
            mountain lion down in the ecotone
            weighing a decision. O

vespertine loper
on a slow hunt where
        the trail trails off, I can't
        see you. I assume you. Unlike most unmanned
            equipment of surveillance, this witness
            processes its live feed sense

by sense: taste of death,
smell of death, the death
        touch, and the sound of death,
        plus night-vision illumination achieved
            by means of a gossamer layer of
            holy tissue beyond the

retina rebounding
the unsettling
        dusk back in a dirty
        beam of thick task light trained on the footpath, as
            God sees us flash before him, double-bathed
            in an insufficient haze

on our trudge back to
the car, so the two
   mountain lion senses
   Timing and Speed interlock in the name of
    Ambush, sense of senses. Sense of senses,
    or Collaboration, as

Ambush is known in
civilization.
   There is a record of
   the transaction, as under a green sea washed
    by a dollar; the color of time is
    green phosphor; it powers this

night-vision camera
and greens film of the
   grand prix. You know the trick.
   You learned it in a closet with a flashlight
    and a cat.

LION FELLING A BULL

I came upon a fragment, one
           anterior lion felling
                one anterior bull. I was in a
museum so can't call
           it life, but here I felt my life come down
                upon my life and have something to say about
the continual downhill grade
           of the path from the ancient marble
                quarry the dark marble

here was quarried from. First with form
           and then with stone, I came in love
                upon a fragment and should have loved the
pressure most. I have a
           mother and a query. I quarreled with
                my father the day my son was born and am the
father now. As a girl I flipped
           over my handlebars flying down
                a different hill every

time. I had a childhood friend named
           Jill and an anti-carjacking
                device called a Club I policed myself
with by thinking hard of
           my membership in and a keen sense of
                the end of belonging. I drove my car into
a house, my house into the earth,
           and I'm grinding the earth into hell.
                I want to be more true

to the material world. The
                wild upon the bull, the chisel
                            upon the wild. But it's either true or
it isn't. How can I
                be more than what I am. I want to stop
                            identifying with the caliper or the
marble, the lion, its marble
                mane, or the meat the lowing cow watched
                            its mate become and be

the altering heat again. I
                stood before the fragment and asked
                            what doesn't want to be whole? I've never
found fragmentation as
                beautiful as objects that survive the
                            fall of civilization intact. Half-lion
felling half-bull, I feel pressure
                in the forms to conclude; a coming
                            storm; electricity

in the air; an intention; but
                whose? I saw crudeness in the wear
                            of the marble and finished in mind with
the crudeness of something
                itself unfulfilled. And then something else
                            was exhumed in Athens. All I needed to see
was an inch of hindquarter of
                lion or bull to love the world to
                            its conclusion but a

second front entirely is
           forming. Mythology is sweet,
                but husbandry is history. The head
of another lion
        rises out of the gridded pit having
            nothing to do with symmetry. A colossal
miscounting of lions felling
        a sole bull. Two irreducible
           lions made of the same

material as me will come
        upon me and the pressure that
           made them makes more of them than it makes of
me. The pressure that makes
        makes more of them than it ever made of
           me. Out of proportion, out of the quarry, great
pressure is forming, a thunder,
        I feel a great pressure positioning
           me. It has no regard.

THE HOUSELIGHTS

            "Anyone who doubted its existence
could walk into the backyard just after
            sunset and see
it," so it was said of the original, but
            to view *Sputnik* in my dining
room I'd have to first invite you
            to dine with us, and I probably will

not, such is my reluctance to try to
            entertain you. I was saying a few
days ago to
            a friend who said he never really uses his
living room that he does when he
            entertains, when *Entertainment*
struck me as the most desolate word I

            ever said, that ever could be said. But
I do not think it has come between us,
            except how a
ghost does when it appears to only one guest at
            dinner. Macbeth is the famous
example here, but he was the
            host and hospitality and enter-

tainment are not the same thing. I just broke
            a word in half; what was it Macbeth said
about the last
            syllable of recorded time? That a severed
flatworm who grows back its head keeps
            all its old memories, even
the ones that seem to signify nothing.

Apropos of that kind of nothingness,
I remember wanting to board the black
          conveyor belt
in the stockroom at the Medimart my father
          managed and ride it back to its
origin. I did not think the
          loop began a few feet away, behind

the strip mall, where the makeup girl who let
          me apply all the lipsticks to my mouth
at once, mud, rust,
          and gold, each smudge a revision of the brick wall
I was led to lean against, leaned
          against the wall flirting with the
truckers of PepsiCo. Now there's a free

          man, said my father once, who owns his own
truck and drives it on his own account. I
          want to know is
the soul free? A loop has no beginning and what
          the makeup girl did on break is
between her and the brick wall. Her
          "break" reminds me that a few sentences

ago I made the crass point of breaking
          "entertainment" at "enter," opening
the word to all
          I do not want to go into, furthermore I
said "Macbeth" in the surgical
          theater, where endless dissection
of regenerating shapes writhing on

the plates inserted beneath the lenses
rotating clockwise above the rising
           mechanical
stage is just the first microscopic violence. Blood
           instructions, as Macbeth put it,
which, being taught, return. Cells, ghosts.
           The flatworm remembers itself. It is

immortal. Macbeth plagues himself. Is this
           as close as we get to the Globe when by
Proclamation
           it was closed? I want to get closer. The closer
I get the more it is closed to
           me. No empty empty as a
stage unentered unexited, except

           an empty house. There is no roof, but the
heavy door is locked. Ramon Fernandez,
           tell me, if you
know, why, when the interminable show we caught
           at the Globe in City Park paused
for intermission, we didn't just
           go home. Fleas were eating us alive, time's

dumb couriers of plague and death. Tempus
           fugit. Fuck it, we said, we're already
here. Sacha and
           Nick were playing with a beach ball just outside the
theater. I don't remember where
           Mary was or who blew up the
ball but whoever of us it was will

never get that breath back. Later, when Nick
and I switched places, as legend has it
          Shakespeare did with
a boy who grew fevered playing Lady Macbeth,
          the beach ball rolled over a dead
squirrel, and I had no recourse but
          to kick it in the road where my son could

not touch it. The ball or the squirrel? Only
          syntax remembers; it's out of my hands
now. What is *it*,
          is one question. The other is where is that child
actor's mother, about which the
          legend of Macbeth says nothing?
She was beside him. Was backstage. She kissed

          him. She thought he had a soul. Knew he did
not. He's not in the folio. His name
          was "Hal." I do
not think he was a real boy, but he had a real
          mother. She was bored sometimes and
sometimes shot through with energy
          of such force she thinks she's God. I have a

dream that comes to me in nothing but voice.
          Imagination enters darkness while
my body rests.
          A scholar-monk could make a word like *prepare* glow
in the dark by suggesting it
          derived by way of pre-paired beasts
milling knowingly near the forlorn dock

because each entry in the lexicon
is a live wire whose root is charged by a
                    holy fire, as
when a cannon shot in a play really burns the
                    theater down. God, I love when the
wall breaks. *No one has to get hurt*
                    means someone is going to get killed. Come,

let's go in together. The houselights are
                    flashing code at us. It's like being winked
at by Bacchus.
                    Yes or no? Yes. That's what entertainment *is*. When
something is between us; holding
                    it there. We will go to terra
with it among us. Something held under,

                    something interred. You'll be lonely if you
say no in a crowded theater. Try to
                    go along with
it. Just go along with it. Entertainment means
                    yes in the dark. It's the curse of
Macbeth. Believe it until the
                    lights come back up and the theater throws us

up, out the vomitoria carved like
                    mighty intestines with archways like hell
mouths through which we
                    exit Giants MetLife Stadium, funneling
out ninety million customers;
                    what customer service, what crowd
control, but there is no such measure out

                    the Forty-second Street Broadway theater
at the site of the old Apollo and
                    Lyric where I
caught *42nd Street* on September 15th,
                    2001. The Saturday
after that Tuesday, that's right; I
                    had tickets. The show, as all shows are, is

about how the show must go on. It was
                    sold out in advance; what are the chances:
not an empty
                    seat in the house. Between acts we roamed the lobby
preparing for something. I am
                    not patriotic, but even
the chorus girls, the ushers, those of us

                    in the dress circle, all cried when the girls
mounted their huge dimes, each on her own tin
                    stand about the
size of the drums upon which elephants balance,
                    and sang, "We're in the money, we're
in the money," because enter-
                    tainment is unbearably sad and so

unlikely, and the human spirit is,
                    and has terrible, gorgeous gams kicking
and kicking in
                    unison. I think you understand I felt sick
telling my friend he *entertains*
                    in his living room and why I
hate poetry and having depicted

this nothing life I live in a field of
mortgaged dust as one in which we drift through
rooms with nothing
to discuss but rooms themselves. My house stood for a
long time before I came in and
tried to make it stand for something.
The sun drips fire. I want to hold steady

in mind, entertain an idea without
it having to arrive. I do not want
you to go, which
is just to say, I hope you won't even come. I
dine beneath the chandelier called
Sputnik alone. *Voyager 1*
exits and enters in the bedroom farce

that is the universe out the solar
system into interstellar space, but
Sputnik, in a
blast of obsolescence, the planned kind, gone in a
ball of flame upon reentrance
into the atmosphere of Earth
from its pulsing orbit through the nothing

that surrounds us from whence my commitment
to atmospherelessness in my dining
room where, as on
the moon, because there is no atmosphere there at
all, no wind, no stirring weather,
first footsteps of men still emboss
the chalky lunar dust, I must leave all

                evidence for all time untouched; ruts where
the legs of chairs slide through the floor polish
                some former home-
owner first measured into the bottle cap then
                poured into the bucket and walked
a mop through underscore the deep
                intentional neglect with which I tend

my *Sputnik*. You want to know my design
                taste, *House Beautiful* or *Elle Decor*, both
of which I sold
                subscriptions to as a telemarketer in
the Midwest in a call center
                with a giant blackboard where our
names were scratched in chalk beside daily sales

                figures? It's pre-reentry dawn, pre-bust.
The show, which has been thrillingly boring,
                about to come
to nothing all the time. The Metropolitan
                Opera House is not more true.
That hothouse raises its ghastly
                *Sputnik*s up slowly as its crystals dim.

Dramatic. But not how it's done in space.
                There is one great lowering. A blast as
silent as the
                silence before and after it. Even fire can
not find its voice in space. All it
                says to me is prepare for more
silence. I'm not special. It says that to

all the girls. I was prepared to attend
a performance of *La Traviata*
                    by a public
high school music teacher who lived at the tip of
                    Manhattan in a borrowed house
so stately its staircase served as
                    the stately staircase set of a private

school in a Woody Allen film about
                    private boredom, because her husband, a
higher-up in
                    the church, received the house as part of his holy
compensation. Preparing for
                    attending *La Traviata*
at the Metropolitan Opera

                    House involved two points: an understanding
that midcentury home design is based
                    entirely
on the principle of moving swiftly so as
                    not to be seen awaiting a
destiny better than this one,

                    followed by the vow to excuse ourselves
if we should find ourselves in a fit of
                    coughing to a
dark recess behind the seating where we were told
                    marble fountains stood waiting for
us, dispensers, too, dispensing
                    conical paper cups you can't put down

that turn a moist white vortex you can crush
                       with one hand, very fulfilling. Who would
believe me? I
                       did have a coughing fit and was grateful for the
preparation to stand excused
                       in the corridor. I stayed there
until the strayed woman died and had to

                       push against the tide of everyone who
was then exiting the theater to get
                       my bag out from
under the seat that had been in front of me. I
                       might be confusing this part with
a flight I once took that made an
                       emergency landing back at the same

airport I departed from. I love you.
                       Do you love me? It will be hard for you.
Everything Goes.
                       I saw that at the Vivian Beaumont across
the plaza from the opera house
                       the day a singer there, someone
unknown to you, backed off the balcony

                       like a scuba diver into the sea
during intermission just after the
                       haunted banquet
where Lady Macbeth sang *fill up this cup* beneath
                       the implicit light of *Sputnik*
in retrograde. I think *Sputnik*
                       is the moon of an unnatural world,

or a god we caught and dangle in a
               cage above our drama, but demanding
the attention
               of a god commands the room. This is all I know:
its name means companion. When my
               family came out the other
theater humming, we saw the lights of the

               emergency, TV crews, we didn't know
what had happened yet, not until later,
               after dinner
where roller-skating waiters served us desperately.
               I was embarrassed. Ill with it.
Back at the Wall Street–money black
               glass apartment of my uncle to which

I'd never been before and to which I
               never would return—this was the leap year
nineteen eighty-
               eight, January 23rd, I had just turned
fifteen—we turned on the news. I
               meant to say *Anything Goes*. Not
Everything. Anything. (Painted portholes)

               (beyond which) not everything, anything
(the horizon, imagined) *Anything*
               Goes. It goes in
dis   crim   in   at   ely.   The rest   of it   is true.

"Gate" and "Fourth of July, 2012" appeared in the letterpress chapbook *Gate*, handmade by Spurwink Press; "H1N1" and "Nursery Furniture" appeared in the chapbook *Novel Influenza*, handmade by the Catenary Press. Grateful acknowledgment is made to the generous editors and artists of both. Additional thanks to all at the following journals, where the poems collected in *A Woman of Property* initially appeared: *Boston Review, Columbia: A Journal of Literature and Art, Company, The Harvard Advocate, The Literary Review, The New Republic, The New Yorker;* the PEN Poetry Series at PEN USA, *Poem-A-Day* at the Academy of American Poets, *Poetry, A Public Space, The Spectator* (UK), and *West Branch Wired.* Thank you to the editors of *The New Census: An Anthology of Contemporary American Poetry,* Rescue Press, for including "H1N1." "The Mountain Lion" is the basis of the short film *DARPA Grand Challenge,* by Nick Twemlow, streaming at *TriQuarterly.*

"H1N1" quotes some of the words and music of *Time for Bed,* by Mem Fox. "Fourth of July, 2012" responds to the discovery at CERN of the so-called God particle on that day.

I am grateful to the Brown Foundation Fellows Program at the Dora Maar House in Ménerbes, France.

Deep gratitude to the dear friends who patiently thought these through with me.

Thank you, Paul Slovak.

These poems are for Nick and Sacha.

NICK TWEMLOW

Robyn Schiff is the author of the poetry collections *Revolver* and *Worth*. Her poems have appeared in *The New Yorker*, *The New Republic*, *Boston Review*, *Poetry*, and elsewhere. Schiff is a coeditor at Canarium Books, and she teaches poetry at the University of Iowa.

JOHN ASHBERY
Selected Poems
Self-Portrait in a
  Convex Mirror

PAUL BEATTY
Joker, Joker, Deuce

TED BERRIGAN
The Sonnets

LAUREN BERRY
The Lifting Dress

PHILIP BOOTH
Lifelines: Selected Poems
  1950–1999

JULIANNE BUCHSBAUM
The Apothecary's Heir

JIM CARROLL
Fear of Dreaming:
  The Selected Poems
Living at the Movies
Void of Course

ALISON DEMING
Genius Loci
Rope

CARL DENNIS
Another Reason
Callings
New and Selected Poems
  1974–2004
Practical Gods
Ranking the Wishes
Unknown Friends

DIANE DI PRIMA
Loba

STUART DISCHELL
Dig Safe

STEPHEN DOBYNS
Velocities: New and Selected
  Poems, 1966–1992

EDWARD DORN
Way More West

ROGER FANNING
The Middle Ages

ADAM FOULDS
The Broken Word

CARRIE FOUNTAIN
Burn Lake
Instant Winner

AMY GERSTLER
Crown of Weeds
Dearest Creature
Ghost Girl
Medicine
Nerve Storm
Scattered at Sea

EUGENE GLORIA
Drivers at the Short-Time
  Motel
Hoodlum Birds
My Favorite Warlord

DEBORA GREGER
By Herself
Desert Fathers, Uranium
  Daughters
God
Men, Women, and Ghosts
Western Art

TERRANCE HAYES
Hip Logic
How to Be Drawn
Lighthead
Wind in a Box

NATHAN HOKS
The Narrow Circle

ROBERT HUNTER
Sentinel and Other Poems

MARY KARR
Viper Rum

JACK KEROUAC
Book of Blues
Book of Haikus
Book of Sketches

JOANNA KLINK
Circadian
Excerpts from a Secret Prophecy
Raptus

JOANNE KYGER
As Ever: Selected Poems

ANN LAUTERBACH
Hum
If in Time: Selected Poems,
  1975–2000
On a Stair
Or to Begin Again
Under the Sign

PHILLIS LEVIN
May Day
Mercury
Mr. Memory & Other Poems

PATRICIA LOCKWOOD
Motherland Fatherland
  Homelandsexuals

WILLIAM LOGAN
Macbeth in Venice
Madame X
Strange Flesh
The Whispering Gallery

ADRIAN MATEJKA
The Big Smoke
Mixology

MICHAEL MCCLURE
Huge Dreams: San Francisco
  and Beat Poems

ROSE MCLARNEY
Its Day Being Gone

DAVID MELTZER
David's Copy: The Selected
  Poems of David Meltzer

ROBERT MORGAN
Dark Energy
Terroir

CAROL MUSKE-DUKES
An Octave above Thunder
Red Trousseau
Twin Cities

ALICE NOTLEY
Culture of One
The Descent of Alette
Disobedience
In the Pines
Mysteries of Small Houses

WILLIE PERDOMO
The Essential Hits of Shorty
  Bon Bon

LIA PURPURA
It Shouldn't Have Been Beautiful

LAWRENCE RAAB
The History of Forgetting
Visible Signs: New and Selected
  Poems

BARBARA RAS
The Last Skin
One Hidden Stuff

MICHAEL ROBBINS
Alien vs. Predator
The Second Sex

PATTIANN ROGERS
Generations
Holy Heathen Rhapsody
Wayfare

ROBYN SCHIFF
A Woman of Property

WILLIAM STOBB
Absentia
Nervous Systems

TRYFON TOLIDES
An Almost Pure Empty Walking

SARAH VAP
Viability

ANNE WALDMAN
Gossamurmur
Kill or Cure
Manatee/Humanity
Structure of the World
  Compared to a Bubble

JAMES WELCH
Riding the Earthboy 40

PHILIP WHALEN
Overtime: Selected Poems

ROBERT WRIGLEY
Anatomy of Melancholy and
  Other Poems
Beautiful Country
Earthly Meditations: New and
  Selected Poems
Lives of the Animals
Reign of Snakes

MARK YAKICH
The Importance of Peeling
  Potatoes in Ukraine
Unrelated Individuals Forming
  a Group Waiting to Cross